BEST PRACTICE IN YOUTH MINISTRY

Edited by Martin Kennedy & Brendan Doyle

Best Practice in Youth Ministry

the columba press

First published in 1998 by
the columba press
55a Spruce Avenue, Stillorgan Industrial Park,
Blackrock, Co Dublin

Cover by Bill Bolger
Origination by The Columba Press
Printed in Ireland by Colour Books Ltd, Dublin
ISBN 1 85607 223 1

Contents

Part 3: Frameworks for Youth Ministry

Introduction

The Tobias Youth Project was set up in 1992 to assist the development of youth ministry in Ireland at local level. It did this by giving a small number of projects modest financial support over four years so they could foster 'good practice' in youth ministry.

The criteria the Tobias Project used in assessing funding applications were as follows:

1. A commitment to the training of, and allocation of responsibility to, lay leaders.

2. A commitment to long term planning and evaluation.

3. Integration of personal development and faith development in the programmes.

4. A willingness to allow any new ideas or programmes be adopted by other groups or parishes.

The Tobias Project has assisted twenty two projects over its four year life. Since the funding of the project has come to an end, the co-ordinators believe that, given the many examples of good practice in the projects, it would be of benefit if the experience and reflections of the groups involved were shared with a wider audience.

With this in mind fourteen projects were selected. They represent a good cross-section of what is happening in youth ministry in Ireland today. They include:

- diocesan youth ministries where the emphasis is on helping and training local parish teams,
- deaneries/regions collaborating together
- individual parish/local initiatives.

The co-ordinators commissioned Colm Ó Muirí to visit each of the fourteen projects in order to interview the leaders and discuss their vision, difficulties, successes and hopes for the future. Martin Kennedy edited the reports and set them in context with an overview of youth ministry in Ireland.

Our thanks to Peter Dorman, Brendan Doyle and Bishop Donal Murray for giving permission to reprint their articles, and to the Catholic Youth Council who originally published them in their quarterly publication *Update.*

We are indebted to all the people and groups who have contributed to the development of youth ministry and have shared their experiences for this publication. We hope that it will further promote good practice in youth ministry in Ireland and beyond.

Brendan Doyle
Martin Kennedy
Kevin O Rourke SJ
Co-ordinators of the Tobias Project

PART ONE

Youth Ministry: An Overview

1. Youth Ministry – the challenge

Most of us who engage in ministry to youth find ourselves at the interface of two very different cultures – the fast-moving world of youth and the slow-moving world of the church. Trying to keep our feet firmly planted in both at the same time is hard. For those who remember a time when church and society moved at one pace and to the one beat, this present situation is especially difficult. Up to and into the 1960s there didn't seem to be any problem. By the 70s this had changed, and now in the 90s changed utterly. Who to blame? Ourselves, youth, the church? The temptation is to scapegoat one or other of these – to say 'I am inadequate', or 'youth are no good', or 'the church is a dead loss'. But that is to make a superficial analysis, and a self-defeating one.

Youth ministry is simply the church caring for the young; seeking to offer, as best we can, the gift of the gospel – Jesus' delightful vision of human possibility. Young people today want a delightful vision of life as much as any other generation. But how we go about offering that gift is the question. Young people are now growing up in a fundamentally different world from that which gave birth to our modern church. Fr Pat Collins CM has summed up a key aspect of this change – *a shift from the experience of authority to the authority of experience*. By this he means that previous generations grew up in a time when authority carried particular weight, and many social agencies – including the church – used authority to deliver their message. I remember as a child being slapped in classroom for not remembering my red dot and blue dot catechism questions. A peculiar way of seeking to pass on the good news of the gospel! But the church got away with that kind of authoritarian behaviour then partly at least because it was a cultural norm. Not so today. People now, and young people in particular, will accept something as good or true or beautiful, not because somebody insists that it is so, but only if they *experience* it so for themselves. Because of our use and abuse of authority in the past (and still, in the eyes of many, in the present), we do have a credibility problem that makes youth ministry especially difficult. A 1995 *Irish Marketing Survey* poll makes this point well. While 44% of people over the age of 65 believed the recent scandals have permanently damaged the church, that figure rises to 75% for those under 34 years of age.

The challenge for us today is to offer young people *delightful* religious experience. That is something we are going to have to learn how to do. We are still as church working largely out of the practices and structures that developed and thrived in a different era. We have to develop new practices and new structures for a new time. This book describes fourteen youth ministry projects that are attempts to do just that. It also seeks to set out in more detail the general context of these ministries and to name their longer term significance. Hopefully, in doing this, it will offer a more energising alternative to the mood of pessimism that is about our church – a mood that can be summed up as this: things were good in the past, they're bad now, and they'll be worse in the future!

2. Situation of young people today

A basic way of caring for young people is simply to pay attention to them. Paying attention to the masses of the young inevitably means looking at statistics. This may not strike us as having much spiritual relevence. Yet statistical analysis in a church context is really a form of meditation – pondering the experience of the young with the question: 'What is God asking us to do and be in this reality?'

A key statistic to begin with is that we in Ireland are part of the first world, where 20% of the planet's population consume 85% of the planet's resources. We are at the receiving end of a profit-making process that exploits the earth's raw materials, converts them into myriads of commodities, and then puts enormous resources into convincing us – aptly named 'consumers' – to buy and consume them. That extraordinary and very destructive cycle of production, promotion and consumption (where so much is fed to so few) needs, at its core, a supportive vision for human destiny if it is to be kept going. And that vision is simply this – we are made for consumer goods, and our hearts are restless until they rest in these! It is a spiritual vision seeking to shape what we believe in, what we hope for, what we love, and it has been described by one historian of cultures, Fr Thomas Berry, as the narrowist since humankind emerged from the early Stone Age. As such it is a very constrained space for something as deep and wide and high as the gospel.

There are one million people between the ages of 10 and 24 in Ireland, and they have grown up in the heart of the First World in a way that was generally not true of previous generations. A number of significant events between the late 1950s and early 1970s set the scene for their very different social and cultural experience. A new government economic policy in 1958 saw a major drive for industrialisation. The opening of a national television station in 1962 (within 4 years 85% of all homes had television) brought a window of the first world into our homes. The introduction of free education in the mid-sixties hugely increased participation in second and third level education. Ireland's entry into the EEC at the beginning of the seventies brought our national income from 60% of EU average to its present 100%.

People born in the 50s and before, grew up in a much simpler, poorer, more rural and insular society. People born after that grew up in an increasingly urban, industrialised, educated, open and rich society. These following figures will look at some of the concrete ways this is effecting the young. The spending power of those in Ireland between 10 and 24 in 1988 was one thousand million pounds per year. That kind of spending power makes them the objects of enormous interest to the commodity producers. In 1993 those producers paid Irish advertising agencies over three hundred million pounds to promote their wares. This included some 646 hours of advertising on RTÉ alone. The following pattern of televiewing among the young is significant in this light.

Figure 1: Average hours of TV viewing by age

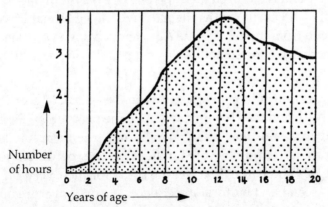

By the age of 12 the average young Irish person is watching four hours of television per day. How can the impact of all this be gauged? An IMS survey in 1988 addressed the question of who (among Irish people) are the favourite personalities of the young. It was an interesting question because who we admire in the world out there says a lot about our inner values. The top ten favourite personalities revealed in the survey were all affluent, successful males, the embodiment of much of the consumer culture dream/fantasy.

The basic point I want to make here is that if we think, as church, that we are the only agency attempting to inculcate the young with spiritual values, then we are very naïve. The spirituality of consumerism is being offered to the whole population in a unceasing and massive way. So if we find that when we bring our gift of the gospel many are not interested, it may mean simply that their hearts and minds are already entranced with another spirituality.

It seems to me too that in justice to the young we cannot explore any aspect of their experience without taking this reality into account. One example here is sexuality. Much of the advertising and imagery directed at the young has a sexual content. At a time in their lives when they are forming their identity and establishing a basic set of values and lifestyle, this cannot but have a significant impact. It is in this context that we need to view the fact that between 1981 and 1994 the percentage of non-marital births to teenagers more than doubled in relation to total births in the country.

Another example is youth crime. While all young people are exposed to the same cultural imperative to consume, one in every four lives in a household below the poverty line. What does it do to their sense of self and society when, on the one hand, they are told that they must be consumers if they are to be anybody, and on the other hand they are systematically denied access to the finances for this? When we look at the statistics of who goes to jail for what, this question needs to be borne in mind. The numbers of people in the 15-25 age group committed to prison rose from 1,494 in 1988 to 1,845 in 1992, an increase of 23%. These are made up massively of people from poor areas and the majority of their crimes are against property, without violence.

No more than with their sexual behaviour, it seems to me that we cannot fairly view or judge young people's anti-social behaviour without looking at the broader social arrangements that influence that behaviour. To focus simply on their own personality, or even for that matter, on their family, is to miss this point. Likewise, we cannot view their relationship with church apart from this wider picture.

3. The church and change

As a church we have not adapted well to the new reality. Religious practice is down on all fronts, particularly among those most effected by the industrial culture – the young, the urban and the unemployed. So in 1991, while 90% of rural employed people were still attending Mass, this figure was down to 40% for urban unemployed. Overall, Mass attendance has fallen from 91% in the 1970s to 66% in the mid 90s, and attendance among these three categories is on average much lower in all the studies. This drop has been accelerating dramatically in recent years and the most recent study (*Irish Times*, December 16, 1996) shows that now only a minority of people born since 1960 still attend Mass. The sharp decline in vocations is another indicator that as church we are less and less able to spark the religious imagination of the young in their new culture.

So, what can we do? Is it inevitable that our contact with the young will continue to decrease in the coming years? Are we helpless in the face of this? I don't think so. Again, as with any analysis of the young, we need to stand back a bit from the church to get a perspective on our situation. Charles Handy's analysis of organisations and the experience of change is particularly helpful here. According to Handy (*The Empty Raincoat*, London: Hutchinson, 1990) organisations exist in continually changing environments, and must continually adapt to change in order to survive. Organisational strategies that emerge and thrive in a given environment will fall into decline as that environment changes. This is pictured in the s-shaped curve (figure 2). For an organisation to survive it needs to throw out a second, experimental curve in anticipation of the coming changes. The experience and insight gained on this second curve will allow the organisation to grow in the new environment instead of decline.

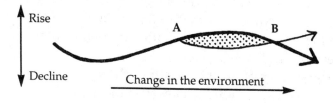

Figure 2: Strategy curve

The high point of the rising curve (a) is precisely the point that a new curve needs to begin in anticipation of the coming decline. The new curve overtakes the old at a point of decline in the old (b), by which time it would have been too late for the new one to begin had it not already started. The new curve seeks to anticipate the new environment and, through trial and error, develops appropriate structures and practices for it. In time it becomes the main curve as the old one declines. The period between the two points is a time of duality, where the past co-exists with the future in the present.

4. The historical context

Applying this model to the church, a number of significant factors emerge. As has been already outlined, the last 30 years have seen the church move into a radically different cultural environment here in Ireland. Yet, while our environment was changing, our pastoral practices have largely remained the same, practices that were introduced in the first half of the last century. They represented at the time a revolutionary change from the Celtic folk practices and spirituality which had predominated up to then. Following the Reformation in England in the sixteenth century, Tudor monarchs carried through a sustained campaign of anglicisation in Ireland that involved numerous attempts at suppressing Catholicism. These efforts included banning of the Mass, execution or exiling of clergy, and confiscation of lands held by Catholics. Many penal laws were enacted, severely disadvantaging Catholics. In 1530 Catholics owned 100% of the land; by 1778 that figure had fallen to 5%. In the early eighteenth century the bounty on a priest was £30, a vicar general £40, a bishop or a Jesuit £50. The impact of all this was that church organisation was reduced to a minimum. However, the faith of the people survived these times – it was articulated then in a tremendous blossoming of popular piety in the form of folk prayers and practices which fed the spiritual life of the people. A collection of 539 of these folk prayers was published in 1974. It shows how prayer was integrated into the daily lives and struggles of the people in a manner that was not dependent on church buildings or clergy.

By the early nineteenth century the last of the penal laws were removed. Catholic emancipation had been granted and the church set about rebuilding itself. A central figure in this rebuilding was Paul Cullen, Rector of the Irish College in Rome who was made Archbishop of Dublin in 1850. The centuries of anti-Catholic legislation had left the institutional church organisationally very weak. A strong tradition of emigration had intensified after the mid-century great famine, resulting in a halving of the Irish population during the nineteenth century. As the bulk of emigration was to English speaking countries, the Irish language went into severe decline, a decline which greatly weakened the tradition of folk prayers. Further, Archbishop Cullen disapproved of the tradition of religious practice which had not been centred around the church building or the priest. His efforts were towards replacing that tradition with one more amenable to clerical control.

One of Cullen's first tasks was to call a Synod of the Irish bishops in Thurles, the first full and formal Synod since the twelfth century. The basic pattern for the future of the church was laid down at Thurles. According to historian Fr Patrick Corish: 'This programme for the new age contained little or anything that was really new. It is hard to find anything at Thurles that was not laid down at Trent (sixteenth century). Hitherto the full Tridentine pattern had been difficult to implement in Ireland. Now it was to go the way of Catholic Europe.' (*The Irish Catholic Experience*)

Mass attendance, estimated at around 30-40% in the 1850s, jumped to 90% within 50 years and stayed that way up to quite recently. There were only 120 nuns in Ireland in 1800. That figure became 8,000 by 1900 and continued to grow right through to the 1970s. By the 1860s there were 2,339 churches in the country, 2,000 of which had been built since the beginning of the century. From the mid-century the extension of state-sponsored social and education systems was gradually and effectively brought under Catholic control by Cullen. Religious instruction took its form from the Tridentine question and answer catechism with emphasis on the Christian life as obedience to concrete rules. The Sunday sermon was the normal supplement to the catechism and was itself supplemented by the parish mission. The parish mission was an intensive week-long programme of religious devotions run by specialist teams of priests. The priests who ran the parish missions (Redemptorists, Passionists, etc) in turn left behind them institutions to nourish a devotional spirituality. The decline of traditional celtic spirituality left a devotional vacuum in the lives of the people. The mission priests filled that vacuum with a flood of imports from the continent – jubilees, tridua, novenas, forty hours, perpetual adoration, blessed altars, benediction, stations of the cross, devotions to the Sacred Heart and the Immaculate Conception, sodalities, societies, scapulars, missals, prayer books, medals, holy pictures and so on. People adopted these with enormous enthusiasm.

Irish Catholicism, thus shaped by Cullen, flourished for the remainder of the nineteenth century and for three quarters of the twentieth century. Now near the end of that century many of the devotional practices have virtually disappeared, the number of seminarians in Maynooth College is at its lowest for over a century, the numbers of religious are declining dramatically, Mass attendence in many urban areas is back to or below mid-nineteenth century levels. Viewed from Handy's perspective, this development is not tragic or disastrous. It is simply another example of the pattern of rise and fall. A particular religious strategy flourished in a particular culture. As the culture changed the strategy became less effective and it fell into decline only in the 1970s as the impact of cultural change began to express itself, particularly on the generation born since the 50s. The challenge is not to recover the past but to develop a new strategy in anticipation of a different future.

According to Handy's analysis, new pastoral practices or experiments should have been introduced in the 60s before the pastoral curve began to decline. That curve is now in steep decline, making experimentation all the more difficult.

5. Youth ministry as experiment

In this context, youth ministry emerges as experimental ministry – an effort at discovering how to offer the gift of the gospel in a new and particularly difficult culture. As experiment it is necessarily slow, messy, incomplete, halting, open to many failures. But it is a sustained effort at gathering wisdom for the church and is part of a much wider curve of experimentation going on in many parts of the church.

There is a crucial question about the relationship between the old and new curves. Seen properly, the new curve does not represent a new, or alternative, or opposition church – but the one church seeking to respond to changing circumstances. Handy makes a point here about this relationship that goes to the heart of the matter. The new curve seeks to gather a wisdom that can revitalise the old. Those on the new curve must seek to offer this wisdom in a manner that the old can understand – and with gentleness. It would be too easy to adopt a superior or condemnatory posture *vis à vis* the old. Those on the old curve, particularly among the leadership, must make space for the new – recognising the significance of its experimentation, being willing to commit financial support. Failure on either side here undermines the fundamental mission of bringing the gift of the gospel to new generations.

Handy's curve allows us to get an energising perspective on youth ministry in terms of the past and the present. We can view the past with respect, but also with a sense of freedom. We don't have to carry the nineteenth century church on our backs into the twenty-first century! We can view the present as a time of adventure – of attempting many new things. Some work, some don't – but we can learn from them all.

There is another element that needs to be added here – to do with the future. On the face of it, Thomas Berry's comment that the consumer culture has brought human imagination to its narrowist since the Stone Age is not encouraging. There has never been a more constrained space within which to bring something of such breadth and height and depth as the vision of Jesus.

Yet the culture too is subject to change. In the face of damage to the environment, war, poverty, oppression of women, and facile spirituality, many within it are questioning its practices and the fundamental values underlying them – third world groups, environmentalists, feminists, justice and peace groups, spirituality groups and others. These are creating space within the culture where the question about values is cherished. In such a space there is enormous possibility for a church that can communicate the gospel.

The church of the twenty-first century can become a delightful, innovative and hugely relevant presence in the lives of the people then. The fact that it is becoming more marginal in the lives of people now should not blind us to this. Seeing the possibilities of the future, being willing to leave the securities of the past, engaging in the adventure that challenges us now – such is a vision of our ministry that can keep our hearts singing in these difficult times.

6. Patterns in the experiment

Learning how to offer the gift of the gospel in our new culture is a challenge that requires the energy and gifts of all who are willing to minister in the church. In our parishes and dioceses we need to create confident, competent teams of people who can engage in ministry, draw wisdom from the engagement, communicate that wisdom – and in all this enjoy what they are at. The Tobias fund was set up to provide some small financial support for groups who sought to engage in youth ministry in this way – with a particular emphasis on planning and training.

Such groups correspond in business jargon to 'high performance teams' – highly motivated, self-directed groups that can function within the broader goals of the organisation. *The One Minute Manager Builds High Performance Teams* (Kenneth Blanchard, Harper Collins 1992) explores the leadership tasks involved in the creation of such teams.

This book throws interesting light on some current practices among youth ministry leaders.

Blanchard recognises four stages in the development of
high performance teams (HTPs) and four corresponding
leadership roles (figure 3).

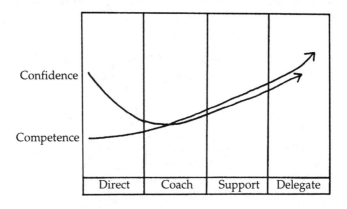

Figure 3

At Stage one the team is beginning – its competence is necessarily low, but its morale may be high if its basic need for
clear direction is met. The role of the leader here is to offer
such direction.

At Stage two the team is engaged in the task and has discov-
ered its lack of experience. Its morale has taken a dent. The
leadership task at this point is very intensive – being with
the team in its task – supporting, encouraging, coaching.

At Stage three, if the team has survived its initial difficulties, its experience and ability will have grown, with a corresponding increase in its confidence. It still needs the support of the leader, but to a significantly lesser extent.

At Stage four the team is at the point where the full responsibility can be delegated by the leader. Leaving go of
the responsibility is crucial. According to Blanchard 'em-

powerment is all about letting go so that others can get going. You will never never never have an empowered self directed team unless the manager is willing to share control.'

How is this put into practice? The following model (figure 4) reflects the approach of a number of youth ministry leaders outlined below.

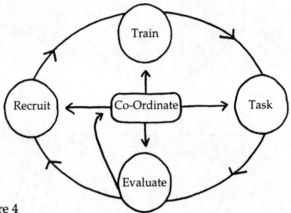

Figure 4

The leader starts by identifying and detailing a clear, limited task, that meets some felt need.

S/he then identifies and details the training that a team of people would need to accomplish that task.

S/he recruits people through an information event where they are given full details of the task and the training. They are invited at the information night to do the training on the understanding that they are free not to do the task if they so chose.

At the end of the training they are invited to do the task and an evaluation of the task.

At the evaluation they are thanked for completing their contract. They are asked for their views on the next step that needs to be taken and are given the option to participate.

A number of those who have completed the task are invited into a co-ordinating role for the next task.

The leader takes on a very directive role at the outset. When the volunteers are engaging in the task for the first time, the leader takes up the coaching role – being with them in the details of the task without doing the task for them. At the end of the task the leader is supporting the volunteers in evaluating and redesigning the task, and is no longer on her/his own at the hub. After a few spins of the wheel the leader is no longer needed at the hub, and can move on to start another wheel, delegating the co–ordination and the task to the volunteers.

7. Practitioners of experimental youth ministry: 14 projects

Parts two and three of this book contain some examples of the practice of youth ministry in this country. They all represent genuine efforts at reaching out to the young in culturally appropriate ways – whether rural, urban or marginalised. All are relatively new, and almost all are working with programmes they developed themselves, or which were developed elsewhere in the last few years.

According to Handy, a key need of people on the second curve is the support and understanding of the organisational leadership on the first curve. Concretely, in church terms, this means the support of the priest/religious or an officially recognised group at parish level, and the bishop at diocesan. Very often people in fulltime ministry are straddling both curves, providing the traditional services to the people and at the same time seeking to develop new ministries. The stories told here highlight over and over again the importance of the supportive role of fulltime ministers for the lay people working on these new ministries.

They also highlight the constant willingness of those in the ministry to try new things – to experiment and then to assess the outcomes. They show how the majority of the experiments are carefully planned and well structured. As such they offer concrete tasks to be done, roles to be taken up. And also the stories highlight the centrality of training.

Something very significant is going on in this. There is a basic recognition that there are people out there who are willing to engage in ministry. What they need is a system of roles and sufficient training to equip them for these roles. The vocation of the people to ministry is being concretely recognised, and the work is being done to find a system of roles and formation for the people. This makes an interesting contrast to our traditional approach to vocations, where our concern has been less to find a system for our people than to find people for our system – that system being the roles of priest and religious and the formation houses of seminaries and novitiates!

As experiments, these are stories in progress – not finished, fixed formulae. They deserve the attention of the church precisely for that – they are indicators of where we might be going in the twenty-first century and of how we might get there.

PART TWO

Fourteen Youth Ministry Projects

1. Kilmore Diocesan Youth Ministry

Background

In 1990 Fr Frankie Kelly, the then part-time Youth Director in Kilmore, published a study of the faith situation of young adults in his diocese. It was the first (and only) such study of its kind in Ireland. Among other things it measured the availability of youth ministry experiences to the young and their openness to the same. A key finding of the study was that a higher percentage of young people expressed openness to youth ministry programmes than had programmes available to them. On the basis of this study, Frankie advocated the establishment of a fulltime youth ministry in the diocese.

Fr Gerry Kearns was appointed fulltime youth director in 1993. He established a house of prayer and welcome, Carraig na Saoirse, with a view to providing prayer and faith experiences for young people from around the diocese. Three years on, he would now place more emphasis on parish-based activities, utilising the house as a resource for that work. His change of emphasis came from the recognition that, without a locally-based youth ministry, what Carraig na Saoirse can provide will only alienate young people from their parishes. His commitment now is to setting up grass-roots youth ministries. His vision is that each parish would have a team of volunteers trained for and committed to the work of local youth ministry. The function of the house is to facilitate this development, providing the training and direction necessary. Key to this is the provision of creative prayer experience for the volunteers, to help them 'move from saying prayers to praying', so that their work of ministry is rooted in and sustained by prayer.

From a practical point of view, this has meant that the primary work of the diocesan team is now with adults rather than directly with the young. However, Gerry feels it is important to have some regular contact with young people. He gets this from being chaplain to a college and being involved on the ground in Cavan town.

Structure

There are two fulltimers based in the house (Fr Gerry and Sr Suzie Duffy) and some 60 trained adult volunteers around the diocese. The house is used to train the volunteers who then work in their own parishes. The fulltimers act as back-up resource to the volunteers. Young adults (18 to 25) and older adults are trained to work with young people in the 12-15 age group. The diocese acquired the house and pays the Director. Income to pay Suzie and cover the expenses of the volunteers comes from fundraising and donations.

Approach

The team first approaches the parishes offering to help set up the *Faith Friends* programme. The priests are asked to call a meeting of parents of confirmation children. The team run the meeting and recruit some parents who are willing to organise the programme. These parents are trained to act as a steering committee. They in turn gather and train young adults in their parish who will be the faith friends to the confirmation candidates.

When the *Faith Friends* programme is finished, the parish team are then offered the *Gift* programmes as a follow-up. Recently two parishes have expanded this approach to include liturgy teams who take responsibility for a youth liturgy once a month.

This approach has led to the setting up of teams of adults in parishes who are trained to run a variety of programmes. Each year some of the experienced parents help train in new parents in their own and other parishes. To date 14 of the 36 parishes in the diocese are involved.

Reflections

Gerry holds that there is a clear value in giving people a definite, limited and achievable task to do in their own area. It offers them a role, and it allows them to take ownership and responsibility for youth ministry in their own parishes. It also allows the parish to see in advance what is being asked of it and what commitment is required. He believes that this approach has greater potential than taking people out of their parishes, giving them a good experience which can leave them powerless and disappointed with their parish experience.

His key concern is the process of forming ministry leaders rather than simply getting this or that programme run. He recognises that this is a slow task. Adults need a lot of encouragement and support. The fulltimers play a crucial role in offering this.

Gerry's experience bears out the results of the 1990 survey. There is a lot of good will on the ground. There are many adults and young people looking for a way to get involved in faith development.

Finally, as the volunteers need nourishment to sustain their commitment, so too do the fulltimers need space for reflection and renewal. A stressed out youth minister is not good for the work!

2. Clonfert Diocesan Youth Ministry

Background

Sr Noreen Lyons was appointed fulltime diocesan youth director in the late 1980s. She works from a youth centre (St Mary's), formerly part of a convent complex in Portumna. Her basic approach to youth ministry is that it belongs properly to the community and her strategy is to enable local communities to develop their own youth ministry. This fits in with her vision of church as people of God, as a community that shows care for all its members, including its young.

Structure

Along with the Director, there are three people working from the Centre on FÁS Community Employment schemes – an administrator, secretary and development worker. There is also a team of some 15 volunteers who work at a diocesan level, training and supporting volunteers involved in youth ministry in their own parishes. The diocese and the Mercy Order make a contribution to the running of the ministry. Other income comes from outside groups using the premises.

Approach

Noreen's basic strategy is to develop a range of youth ministry packages, and to train diocesan teams who in turn train parish teams to run these packages. Key here is a continuous process of evaluating the packages – an evaluation that includes all the participants – which results in the continuous rewriting of the packages in the light of experience. All the youth ministry material being used in Clonfert has been substantially written there. Some 16 of the diocese's 24 parishes are presently involved in this process and four of its seven second level schools.

Gift and *Faith Friends* are two staple programmes in this process. Originally teams were gathered and trained as trainers for the published programmes. As their confidence and competence grew, these teams were able to take on more and more responsibility, and are now at the stage where they can rewrite the materials themselves in the light of the evaluations. Drug abuse, for example, has been written into the *Gift 3* programme this year. Noreen has been able to reduce her involvement in these programmes as the teams took on more.

A programme on emigration was developed in the same way. An initial package was put together to meet a strong need in the late 80s. A team of volunteers were then trained to operate that package. Having initially piloted the package in one school, the team then went on to service all the second level schools in the diocese, continually modifying the material in the light of experience. Now as the emigration situation is changing, a new programme is being piloted with the assistance of a woman on a CE scheme. It is broadly a lifeskills programme aimed particularly at young people who feel marginalised by the points system. Noreen's intention here is that, once the package is developed, a team of volunteers will be trained to operate and modify it.

Apart from providing ready-made packages, Noreen is happy to work with parish groups in the development of their own material in the light of their own needs. Last year one parish group went through a custom-made six-night training programme on youth ministry. As a result they developed and ran their own programme for youth in the parish. This year there are two parishes engaged in a similar process.

Along with stressing the importance of lay formation and the continuous evaluation of material, Noreen also stresses the value of networking with other youth agencies. This includes youth ministry teams from around the country and also the Galway Youth Federation (GYF), whose brief includes the Clonfert diocese. Noreen has found it very enriching of her work to develop links with GYF, to deepen mutual understanding and to look for practical areas of co-operation. The emigration and lifeskills programmes are some of the concrete outcomes of this co-operation.

Reflections

The values of formation, evaluation and networking are central to Noreen's approach to her work. They seem to her to provide a basis for making youth ministry experiences available to the widest possible number of young people.

It is her experience too that, by and large, local groups of volunteers need at least the passive support of local clergy, and where this is absent the groups generally do not survive. She is clear that a diocesan agent cannot provide this local support role, and so concentrates her efforts on parishes where there is a basic openness among the clergy.

In her work with the diocesan volunteers she puts as much emphasis on confidence building as on the details of the programmes. Self confidence is vital in the difficult territory that is youth ministry – confidence to give others confidence to engage with youth, confidence to rework programmes in the light of how these programmes are experienced by the young and the adults.

Finally, Noreen sees the need to have a diocesan policy on youth ministry integrated with an overall diocesan pastoral policy. Towards this end she has gathered and is presently working with a small group who will present a policy document to the bishop. Her hope is that this document will reflect the experience and insights gained from youth ministry both in her own diocese and across the country, and that it might also usefully inform the broader thrust of diocesan pastoral policy.

3. Dromore Diocesan Youth and Prayer Ministry

Background

The ministry began when a Parish Youth Club in Newry organised a *Discovery* programme. Local curate, Peter Devlin, was involved. He followed up the programme with a visit to Teach Bríde in Carlow (a diocesan house of welcome for young adults). When the group returned they set up a prayer room in the club and organised discussion and prayer sessions. A trip to Taizé led to the establishment of Taizé prayer groups around the town of Newry. This was the beginnings of volunteers emerging, peer ministry and ownership, which are key elements of the present day ministry. In 1989 Peter was appointed Diocesan Youth Director. A house of prayer and welcome was set up in Omeath, based on the Teach Bríde model. The programme of activities at the time included weekends and school retreats, *Discovery* programmes in parishes, Easter celebrations in Omeath and specific events to nourish volunteers. With ongoing assessment and outside facilitation, the programme has been changing over the years. In 1990 one of the volunteers was taken on to work fulltime with Peter. In 1993 the ministry base moved across to the other side of Carlingford Lough, to Seafield House in Cill Eoin. In August 1996 Ann Farren was appointed Youth Director and Peter availed of a sabbatical in the USA.

Structure

Peer ministry fundamentally shapes the structure here. All the youth ministry programmes are planned, organised and run by teams of young volunteers (with the exception of school retreats). Four teams respectively run school retreats, weekend retreats, prayer and welcome ministry and parish outreach. A fifth team – adult prayer – has emerged from this ministry in recent years and now works in close association but independently of the youth ministry programme. Two further teams work on the training

and co-ordination of the volunteers. The teams are ser-
viced by the director, a secretary and a youth worker.
Finances are raised mainly by covenant. Dromore Youth is
registered as a charity and run by a Board of Trustees.
These fund the ministry, hire staff and monitor the general
thrust and direction of the ministry. They function as a
support and advisory group for the director.

Approach

Young people offering young people experiences of prayer
and welcome is at the core of this ministry. The young volunteers are organised and facilitated in groups according
to the ministry they want to engage in. Each year the
teams are reformed and new members are brought on
board. This is necessary because of the high turnover in
this age group. People are finishing school and going on to
college or to work elsewhere.

At a planning weekend each September, the teams are
facilitated to determine their agenda and targets for the
year. Each January a mid-year assessment weekend is
held. The teams review their plans, what they have actually
achieved, what difficulties are arising etc., and, in the light
of this, plan their actions up to the summer. In June of each
year an evaluation weekend is held – the year is reviewed
and celebrated, learnings and achievements are noted. A
date for the September meeting is fixed and new people
are earmarked for the teams.

The school retreat team consists of the two fulltime workers and two volunteers. They generally do two retreats a
week. The weekend retreat team consists of some 20 volunteers who subdivide to cover at least one event per
month. Their primary focus is on school and parish groups
who are interested in a local follow-up. The prayer and
welcome team run a weekly prayer meeting as a follow up
option for those who have done the retreats. Most of the
new team members each year are recruited from those

who attend this. The parish team does outreach work to parishes, using mainly such programmes as *Faith Friends, Gift, Discovery* and *Taking Charge of Your Life!* – a youth assertiveness programme. The adult prayer group consists of some thirty volunteers who organise *Enjoy Praying* programmes, scripture programmes and weeks of directed prayer in parishes. A training team organises events to provide skills training for volunteers and team co-ordinators. A co-ordinating team (Le Chéile) is made up of a representative of each of the teams. Here information is shared, events co-ordinated and operational decisions taken. The support and advisory group is made up of former members of the ministry teams and some adults with some expertise in finance, administration and ministry. This group is legally responsible for the ministry and sets its overall policy and direction. In any year the teams generally organise over 100 separate programmes.

Reflections

Anne has only arrived in recent months as Director of the ministry, having had no previous involvement in Dromore. She feels the practice of bringing in outside facilitators for overall ministry planning and assessment has worked well, allowing for a fairly smooth transition of Directors.

A real strength of the ministry is its lay ownership, reflected in its structure of teams, its funding through covenanting by interested individuals, and its ownership by a group of trustees. All this seems to her to be a very concrete expression of lay involvement and commitment.

However, she feels that this very definite structure has its disadvantages – making it more difficult for people to move beyond their familiar activities. For instance, she would like to see a greater involvement with more marginalised groups, but it may take the development of some definite programme to facilitate this.

4. Oblate Youth Support Group, Dublin

Background

This is an umbrella group made up of representatives from six areas of Oblate ministry – four parishes, a school and a retreat centre. (The Oblates are a Religious Order based in Dublin.) It originated from a series of reflection days among the Oblates in those areas. The support group was established in 1990 with the aim of supporting those in youth ministry in the areas where Oblates are involved, by providing a forum where experience can be shared, new ideas generated, new projects developed and training resources organised to meet the needs that arise.

Structure

There are three levels to the structure here. At the first level, two reps from each of the six areas meet twice a term to provide support and co-ordination. At the second level, each of these reps belongs to an area youth ministry team. At the third level, the teams are operating on the ground a comprehensive programme of planned, sustained youth ministry activities that touch some hundreds of young people in the 7-18 age group.

Approach

The basic purpose of the forum is to provide a system of peer support for the adult leaders of the various youth ministries. Here they can swap ideas, advice, encouragement, etc. Beyond this the forum will also initiate joint actions to meet common needs that arise – particularly training needs. Each of the six youth ministries operates independently, but the forum provides the space for occasional collaborations.

The kinds of ministries taking place in the areas include *Faith Friends*, children's choirs, folk groups and youth liturgies, Cycle of Care, peer ministry programmes in the school, youth pilgrimages to Lourdes and others. In the Cycle of Care some areas use particular programmes to maintain the ongoing contact with the youth. Others have developed a more informal strategy using a variety of one-off events like hikes, school days, etc. About 50 students in the 11-17 age group have been involved in a faith development project in the school (Belcamp) which includes leadership training. This has led to a peer ministry outreach among the students.

The training activities facilitated by the forum included a series of workshops for the youth leaders from the different areas. These covered personal and faith development, leadership skills and styles, and how to motivate young people and leaders. They also included a programme for folk groups and a workshop on scripture through drama and music (run by the National Bible Society).

Reflections

The forum has met a strong felt need for support among those involved in youth ministry. Its collaborative approach to the training of youth and adult leaders has proved very practical and workable. It has, on the whole, maintained and developed energy for youth ministry in the areas without becoming a burden for those involved.

5. Tullamore Parish Youth Initiative

Background

In 1994 the parish employed a fulltime pastoral co-ordinator, Shay Claffey. His wide-ranging brief included youth ministry. He quickly saw the need for a more planned and comprehensive approach to youth ministry in the parish and set about establishing that in his second year.

Structure

A co-ordination group was established consisting of Shay Claffey, a curate, a parish sister, a youth worker employed by the Tullamore Community Services Council (who was also supervising a Community Employment Scheme), and an outside facilitator with a background in youth ministry. This group met a number of times during the year to agree, implement and monitor a youth ministry strategy.

Approach

As each member of the group was already heavily committed in their work, they adopted the following principle: we will only initiate youth programmes where there are teams of adults ready and willing to take responsibility for those programmes. In the light of this the following approach was planned.

1. Organise an information night on youth ministry programmes for interested adults/young adults. Invite those present to 'sign up' for programmes of their choice, i.e. to join committees who will run the programmes.

2. Provide training for whatever committees emerge from the night.

3. Run only with those programmes that have viable teams to take responsibility for them.

4. Arrange for an end-of-year evaluation and celebration night for the teams.

Following this approach, the co-ordinating group put a lot of energy into recruitment for the information night. A group of 60 people turned up. A two track approach to youth ministry was presented that night. On one track, there were a number of specific programmes including *Faith Friends, Gift,* and a programme for working with youth at risk. On the other track was a listening survey proposal – a method of finding out the felt needs of young people as a first step in developing some community responses to those needs. Sufficient numbers signed up for *Faith Friends,* youth at risk and the listening survey. The numbers for *Gift* proved not to be viable, so it wasn't run at that stage. The youth at risk group did an extensive training programme with the youth worker. Following the training, the group ran a week-long summer programme and once-off follow-on events for young people identified as at risk. Over 50 young people became involved for the full programme. Most of these would never have belonged to any group or club before.

The listening survey committee numbered 14. They were divided into 7 teams of 2. Each team was trained to facilitate a small group of young people over a four night listening survey programme. This simply involved a one hour meeting per week where the young people were asked to talk about issues that they heard young people of their own age talk about with strong feelings – in other words, they talked about what young people their own age were angry about, sad about, delighted about, worried about, etc. The purpose of the survey was to identify issues that the young people felt very strongly about, so that programmes could be put on offer that would be relevant to those needs.

Following the listening survey a public meeting was called to announce the results and explore relevant and feasible responses. Issues that emerged from the survey included difficulties in communicating with adults, boredom, drugs, alienation from church (but not necessarily from God), exam pressure, peer pressure. Again the meeting was run on the basis that only those programmes would run that had sufficient numbers of adults to take responsibility for them. On the basis of this, three committees emerged for three programmes – a youth Fairs Day, a Taizé prayer meeting and the *Gift* programme. There has been a follow through on all three fronts. The Fairs Day featured a range of local sports, leisure and social organisations putting up stands outlining what they had on offer for young people. The event attracted a lot of young people and made headlines in the local paper.

The evaluation and celebration event was then held in May 96. An upshot of the meeting was the formation of a new group to continue the overall work of Tullamore Youth Initiative in the following September.

Reflections

Shay Claffey felt that the basic strategy of running only with programmes for which their was adult commitment worked well. It was a very concrete way of offering adults in a community responsibility for ministry to their young. It also meant that an already overworked parish staff were not further burdened with having to organise and run programmes. Instead they could put their energy into the overall co-ordination. They employed an outside facilitator to provide the training, which over the year cost just under one thousand pounds.

The parish youth ministry initiative also meant liaising with others in youth work – the local youth service, the Community Services Council and the Tullamore Travellers Movement. This was supportive and energising for all the groups concerned.

The year showed that a planned co-ordinated approach to

youth ministry can lay the basis for a comprehensive ministry. However, a crucial need here is somebody to take up the co-ordination role. Shay has since moved from parish co-ordinator to co-ordinator of adult religious education, moving him out of his youth ministry role. As well as this, the youth worker's brief revolves more around supervising the Community Employment Scheme. While the group which emerged from the Tullamore Youth Initiative evaluation and celebration in May 96 is in place, the absence of a fulltime person to take up a supportive and co-ordinating role has seriously restricted the effectiveness of the initiative. This issue is currently being addressed on a number of fronts.

6. Kairos House, Sandyford, Dublin

Background

Kairos House is a privately owned bungalow in Sandyford, Dublin. Its owner, Geraldine Glasgow, has made it available as a centre for personal, creative and spiritual growth for young people and adults. She continues to live in the house, works as a consultant and facilitator for church and business groups, and dedicates the rest of her time to ministry in her own home. Geraldine began this work in 1980. A *Jill* programme was run in the parish and afterwards Geraldine invited the group to meet in her house on a weekly basis. Her ministry has developed since then and the house is now in use four nights and one morning per week, and on occasional weekends. The first twelve years of this ministry happened in her home in a nearby housing estate in Wedgewood. That became too small for the demands being made on it. With an interest-free loan raised by the local community, she bought a derelict bungalow in Sandyford village. 114 volunteers worked on the house over a month to get it into shape. Its facilities include three sitting rooms and a prayer room, all with turf fires!

Structure

Geraldine provides the co-ordination and inspiration for this ministry. A large number of volunteers provide back-up support such as accounting, transport, counselling, social work, legal advice, carpentry, plumbing, etc. These are drawn from the 600 or so people who have had a deep involvement in Kairos over the sixteen years. Geraldine works with young people from the age of 14 up. Generally they maintain a regular contact with the house for three years or more, and are then encouraged to move on to other things – further education, training, etc. Paid facilitators work with a variety of groups, costing Geraldine about £4,000 per year. Donations, fund-raising and voluntary contributions help to cover these costs (£3 for working adults, £1 for young adults, 50p for teenagers).

Approach

The house provides a range of programmes covering three areas of development – personal, creative and spiritual. Geraldine believes the three are closely connected and work in one naturally leads to work in others. A typical programme for the young would include assertiveness, art and meditation. There are also men's and women's groups, retreats, workshops and open days. Every December group activities stop and everybody helps with the Toys Project, involving the collection and distribution of toys all over the city. There is a room for homeless young people to sleep while they await more permanent accommodation. There are a number of trained counsellors that Geraldine can refer people to as the need arises. A lot of one-to-one counselling goes on in the house as well as a bereavement service.

Reflections

The approach, initially quite informal and unstructured, has evolved into a definite pattern and structure. Geraldine feels that this has been positive, allowing young people definite activities while building positive relations with adults. The lack of structure at the beginning was chaotic. An integral part of the structure is keeping the house empty every Friday and for three months during the summer.

The atmosphere of the house is homely and relaxed – turf fires and home-made bread help here! In such an atmosphere it is easier to create a sense of ease where the young people – particularly those from difficult backgrounds – are able to share and find a listening ear.

It is Geraldine's experience that people hunger for spirituality, if it is presented in a digestible form. Here she finds that personal development and artistic programmes provide doors into the spiritual. And when adults are touched by this, it has a positive impact on their whole family.

Why does she do it? Geraldine works from deep religious convictions which include a reverence for the dignity of people – a reverence that has opened her to a spirituality that is concerned with the development of the whole person. Such a spirituality has proven very attractive to the people who encounter it.

7. FACE: Finglas Youth Initiative, Dublin

Background

FACE is a community youth movement based in Finglas. Its primary focus is to engage local young people in caring and in justice activities. The movement began in 1989 after Fr Denis Collins brought a group of young people from Coláiste Eoin, a local secondary school in Finglas, on an exchange with a Catholic Youth Organisation in Canton, Mass., USA. They spent a month in the States where they did voluntary work with old folks, in hospitals, etc. They so enjoyed the experience that on their return they set up a youth group modelled on what they had seen in the US. FACE stands for Finglas And Canton Exchange.

Structure

The movement presently consists of some 70 young people from the second level schools in the area, along with adult and young adult leaders. There are 8 working groups and a co-ordinating committee. Each of the groups has a specific outreach – social service, friends of remedial clinic, youth club, big brother/big sister programme, human rights, newsletter, Northern Ireland, etc. One of the groups is comprised of members of FACE who have gone on to college, but who have maintained links with the movement, offering support and leadership to the younger members. The co-ordinating group meets on a monthly basis. Its members each belong to one or other of the working groups. FACE has its own constitution. It has recently finished a five year plan and has another three year plan prepared. Its running costs come to £10,000 per year. Members do most of their own fund-raising. The Irish American Fund and Comhairle have also provided funding. The CYC, Greenpeace and Finglas Youth Service have provided training for the members.

Approach

The basic thrust of the movement is to train young people to run their own organisation and take their own actions. The five year plan was drawn up covering all the activities. This was then incorporated into the programmes of the different groups. Training events are offered to the young to equip them for these activities. Fun events, planning events, weekends away and religious events are also part of the life of the movement.

The social services group do a lot of work with elderly in the community. Each member of the big brother/big sister group adopts as a friend for a year a young teenager who has experienced some difficulty. The human rights group in the last year has organised an overnight protest outside the British Embassy in connection with British-made weapons being exported to Indonesia for use in East Timor. They looked after 20 Chernobyl children during a summer camp, organised summer programmes for the Bosnian refugees in the local Cappagh hospital, lead the Amnesty International protest on Brazilian street children, took part in a Sellafield protest, organised a Greenpeace gig involving local bands, and took part in numerous other activities.

Other groups are involved in outreach to the disabled and the disadvantaged. The US exchange continues on a yearly basis. The Irish North-South exchange has been working very well.

Reflections

For adult leader Denis Collins, the key to FACE is giving young people ownership. Educating young people to run something is better than doing it for them. They grow in confidence and there is more energy and creativity all around. It avoids dependency on a few adult leaders, leadership burn out and the collapsing of the organisation. The young people taking on responsibilities offer models for the younger ones coming up. It is his experience that young people in oppressed areas easily identify with oppression in other cultures. For adult leader John Hughes, the structured and planned approach of FACE has been a huge success. Offering young people an opportunity to be of service in their own community, and to explore other cultures, has sparked their imaginations.

8. Anawim: Priorswood Youth Ministry Group

Background

Anawim is a youth ministry movement with a core group of some 10 young leaders (aged 17-18) who work with younger people in their community. Its aim is to foster the spiritual growth of its members, leading to Christian action in the community, particularly among the young. The group originated from a charismatic prayer meeting organised in their own home by a local couple in 1986. They had teenagers of their own and wanted to reach out to other teens. Young people were invited to meet on a weekly basis in the house to discuss their own experiences and issues and to pray together. The young felt strongly that there was little for young people in the area and decided that they would do something about this. Since then some 300 young people have been members of Anawim. There are around 2000 young people in the 12-25 age group in the area. Most do not belong to any group or club.

Structure

Five of the older members are the elected leaders and two adults provide backup support. The group is supported by the local parish, former Anawim members and the locally-based Religious Sisters of the Sacred Heart. It meets in the parish church. The Sisters funded a fulltime worker for a period and continue to fund one of their own members, Eileen Lawless RSCJ, who provides backup support for the group. Finance also comes from a Comhairle grant, some fund-raising and some EU grants.

Anawim liaised closely with PDR in the parish initially. The CYC has helpd them in their planning and formation of leaders.

Approach

The Anawim group reach out to other young people in a number of ways – including their weekly meeting, the

Faith Friends programme, youth liturgies (with folk group, dance and drama) and football competitions. They bought a mobile home in a holiday resort which serves as a spirituality centre for the group, and especially the leaders. It has also been available to some families in need in the area. They also hold a weekly prayer meeting attended by a group of 15 younger teenagers whom the older group hope will provide continuity for Anawim. As part of the prayer meeting, the young people share their experiences and struggles.

The Anawim group itself goes away regularly on weekends, primarily for sustenanance, but also for planning and reflection. They go for a week's holiday/retreat each summer. They have also had an exchange with a Spanish group. The five members of the leadership team plus Eileen now form part of Priorswood youth ministry team along with other members of the parish and the CYC.

Reflections

The situation for young people in the area is very difficult, with drugs and violence quite prevalent. Eileen believes that young people need to belong to a group if they are to be supported in their choice of an alternative lifestyle. As a support person for Anawim, she sees it as vital that young people in the area have older teenage models, male and female, with whom they can identify, and a group to which they can belong.

The weekly meetings, the *Faith Friends* programme, the youth liturgies and the summer exchanges have proved concrete and effective means of enabling young people to do this modelling. Bringing local young people to Spain provided a great opportunity for training and education that enabled and equipped those young people to take up leadership roles with Anawim. Bringing Spanish young people into the area brought financial and social benefits to the area and led to some high profile youth activities in-

volving the visitors. For Eileen the key to maintaining this
kind of involvement among the young is the training and
support of the young leaders.

9. St Pappin's Youth Centre, Ballymun

Background

In 1987 a parish priest in Ballymun, Kevin O Rourke SJ, decided to integrate the various bits of youth ministry going on in the parish into a single more comprehensive programme. He was looking for a structured way of providing on-going contact with the young. In 1989 he integrated the prayer ministry to primary school children, the activities of the local youth centre, the *Discovery* programme and the *Faith Friends* programme into what subsequently became known as the *Cycle of Care* model, now being used extensively around Dublin. There is close co-operation with the primary school in this. Basically what happens here is that the children involved in the prayer ministry, along with all other children in the school, are invited to do the *Faith Friends* programme, with fifth-year students as Confirmation Faith Friends. These children are then invited to join the youth centre, where their former faith friends are now their youth leaders. The centre runs weekly programmes for each age group from sixth class to sixth year. The programme for the older groups is modelled on the *Discovery* programme. So a child enters this system at as early as three or four years of age through the childrens' prayer meeting, then moves to the confirmation *Faith Friends* programme, follows through with the youth centre programme over the next five years, and then becomes a faith friend to the 12-year-olds entering the system – thus the *Cycle of Care* – those cared for become in time the carers.

Structure

150 young people belong to the groups, with some 26 leaders and an advisory group of 8, one of whom is employed part-time. All leaders meet once a month. They also do up to five training and development weekends each year along with some training courses organised by the local youth service. Funding is raised though a covenanting

system. The sponsors receive regular updates on developments in the ministry. Comhairle also provides some funding.

Approach

Recreation and education are the twin wheels that drive this ministry. Each member belongs to a club of 15 or so that meets weekly. Football, pool, arts, crafts, drama and cooking are integrated with retreats and discussions. These discussions cover the *Discovery* topics – drugs, alcohol, relationships, faith, family, etc. – in a manner suited to the age group. The leaders decide on the most appropriate way of working with their clubs and they are encouraged to be creative in this. A summer holiday is organised for the members each year. To qualify for the holiday, members must attend the weekly club, pay their subscription and generally be well behaved. The holiday also includes a mixture of education and recreation.

All the leaders are drawn from the club membership, and each gets an award each Christmas in recognition of their commitment and contribution.

Reflections

For adult leader, Evelyn Murphy, the vision of this youth ministry is summed up as 'the older ones looking after the younger ones'. She believes that the clear focus and structure of the project, and the atmosphere of warmth and welcome, has made it very attractive to the young. Their policy of training emerging leaders within the project has paid off well, allowing for continuity of the project even with a changeover in personnel.

The policy of consistent rewarding of behaviour and commitment has led to increased standards of behaviour and commitment. This has benefited both leaders and members.

10. Tallaght Travellers Youth Project, Dublin

Background

The aim of this project is to provide an educational and social outlet for Traveller girls. It was established four years ago by a teacher in a Travellers' training centre. It was set up because the girls had very little to do. Generally Traveller parents take a very protective approach to single young daughters and allow them less freedom than is normal for settled girls. The project began when the girls were asked to be faith friends. It has developed since into a number of activities.

Structure

There are ten members in the group and a co-ordinator. The group sets its own targets for its activities every three months. It meets on a weekly basis in a resource centre located on their site. The location was important in getting the permission of the parents. The CYC supply funding to the group to match the Tobias grant.

Activities

They have organised a trip to Knock shrine and a weekend away in Kilnacrott outdoor activities centre in Cavan. This latter was a particular achievement in view of the general restrictions on this group. They have done art and craft classes, have taken part in an environmental awards project, and have interacted with youth clubs from the settled community. Personal development work and social outings are also part of the programme.

Reflections

It took over a year for the co-ordinator to build up trust with the parents to allow the girls to get involved. But that trust is there now and it has allowed for a great expansion in the lives of the girls. The interaction of this group with settled youth groups has also worked well. Each meeting is carefully planned and a numbers balance is maintained between Travellers and settled. Overall the project has had a very positive impact on the members, and many have moved on to training programmes, women's groups, etc.

11. St Matthew's Parish Faith Development Programme, Ballyfermot, Dublin

Background

This is a *Discovery*-like faith development programme for senior secondary school students run by the parish with the support of teachers. It was initiated last year by the local curate who is school chaplain, in conjunction with a CYC faith development worker. Participants were recruited from the two secondary schools in the parish and 50 young people in all were involved.

Structure

Three groups met one night per month for discussion and prayer – a fifth-year, a sixth-year and a past pupils' group. Six teachers volunteered to work with the groups in pairs. The venue was a side room in the local church, and afterwards the groups moved to the presbytery for refreshments and informal chat. The organising team, composed of the curate and teachers, met once a month to review and plan the ministry.

Approach

A series of topics were offered to the groups under three headings – social, personal and spiritual. The groups were asked to chose two from each category. Meetings began with an input from a guest speaker, followed by discussion and then concluded with prayer. Apart from these meetings, retreats and social outings were organised twice a term.

A number of developments have followed from this. The profile of the parish has risen among the young, a number have become involved in parish teams, and a group of 80 turned up for a parish retreat. A group has established a parish newsletter for young people – it was published five times during the year. The chaplain and the teachers began an outreach to past pupils studying in colleges around the country. They visited a number of colleges, invited the past pupils to a meal and a drink, and visited some digs. The chaplain and staff have reorganised the senior religion programme into a modular format, with teachers volunteering for their choice of module. A leadership training programme has also been introduced, including a retreat that explores leadership in the Christian community.

Reflections

The programme started with 12 participants and grew from there by reputation. For school chaplain, David Lumsden, the initial meeting was crucial. The atmosphere of welcome and acceptance, and giving the young a choice in what would be covered, helped to win over the initial group. The use of guest speakers brought a freshness to the discussions. From the parish point of view, he sees an increase in parish participation by the young. For the teachers, there is a noticeable increase in participation and interest in the religion classes. David sees the programme helping to build links between the schools and the parish. It co-ordinates and compliments what is happening in youth ministry in both places and it helps the young move smoothly from one to the other.

12. Darndale Adventure Group, Dublin

Background

This is an imaginative programme of activities geared at the whole development of young people – physical, social, spiritual, mental. In an area where young people are at risk from many pressures – drugs, drink, IRA recruitment, money lending, crime bosses, poverty – this programme seeks to create an enjoyable, challenging and learning environment that can help the young to grow and play a constructive role in their community.

Structure

There are 50 members, 30 of whom are regulars. They meet once a week for three hours, and go away for a weekend every two months. There is a management committee of 6 along with a members committee who are being groomed for leadership in the group. Members of the committees go away for a special weekend every year to review and plan the group activities. The group have the use of a local community hall for their meetings, have access to a Garda community minibus for travel, and use Kilnacrott house and CYC centres for weekends away. Some of the leaders have taken part in CYC and National Youth Council training events. Members pay 50p per week.

Approach

The programme of activities runs on a four week cycle. Week 1: indoor games and activities – pool, football, etc. Week 2: outdoor activities – a night walk in the mountains, etc. (A Garda community minibus is available for these nights.) Week 3: education night – sometimes with guest speakers and small group discussion on topics of interest. Week 4: special interests – quiz, bingo, board games, demonstration on car engines, etc. Every two months there is the weekend away. The weekends are a mixture of outdoor and educational activities.

Along with these activities the group have undertaken a number of projects. They organised three street theatres during Central America Week and One World week, writing the play themselves. The topic was Third World debt, one they could easily understand themselves given the prevalence of money lenders in the area. They have taken part in a Co-operation North exchange with an East Belfast group. They have recently acquired a computer and some are now learning word processing. Some of the members have started groups for some of the wilder elements in the area – a joy riders' group, a young men's group, a women's group. Cookery and swimming classes have also been organised.

Reflections

For leader, Gary McDarby, the project is about 'lighting a candle in the monster's lair'. He and the other leaders work from Christian values and seek to offer these to the young. Much of the discussion about values and spirituality is informal, arising naturally in the context of the activities. Gary finds that while there is a resistance in the group to organised religion, there is an openness to spirituality and to practical Christianity. Hence the actions around Third World issues, joy riding, etc.

13. St Peter's Parish Youth Ministry, Lurgan

Background

Youth ministry in the parish started with a *Discovery* programme run by a local curate and a married couple. They had attended a liturgy course in Carlow and decided on doing something with youth. The following year, with a second couple, they organised a *Love Matters* programme and confirmation *Faith Friends*. They recruited more adults and young adults to help run an expanded range of programmes and organised themselves as a core youth ministry team. Their vision was to involve young people in community and church, to offer them an experience of being church family, to help them develop as well-rounded people.

Structure

The ministry developed over a five year period. The core group met on a regular basis to review and plan their ministry. Training was provided for programme leaders who generally worked in pairs – an experienced person and a newer person. Youth Link Northern Ireland provided some of this training. Funding came initially from the leaders' own pockets; later fund-raising events were organised. The Tobias grant was the only outside financial support. Much of the youth ministry was connected with the liturgy, and the support of the local clergy was crucial in this.

Approach

A range of programmes were run including *Discovery, Make Me A Channel of your Peace, Faith Friends, Love Matters, Growing up Sexually* and Advent programmes. The leaders visited the local schools promoting the programmes and recruiting participants. Much of the youth ministry was linked to Sunday liturgies. A gift liturgy involved primary school children bringing gifts for those in need, and these gifts formed part of the offertory procession. Youth liturgies were organised during Advent and a service called Women Around the Cross was held on Good Friday. Part of the *Make Me a Channel of Your Peace* programme involved a group project. One of the projects undertaken was the setting up of a creche facility for Sunday Mass.

The *Growing Up Sexually* programme involved the particiation of parents of the young. Primary school children visited old folks as part of one of their programmes. Fun cycles were organised in the summer. Some of the programmes were run in people's homes.

Reflections

The whole ministry was built on the commitment and enthusiasm of a small team of lay people supported by the local clergy. They gradually developed in confidence and experience over the years and felt their commitment was well rewarded by the enthusiasm and appreciation of the young. Their pattern – action followed by reflection followed by action – allowed for a steady development in the ministry, for the learning of lessons and the application of those learnings.

But the project came undone when all the clergy in the parish changed within a year. There was no continuity in the youth ministry policy in this changeover, and the lay people suddenly found themselves without the active support of the priests. Indeed they felt that their youth ministry programme was now perceived as a burden by the clergy. The shift from being believed, supported and encouraged in their commitment to being perceived as a burden was devastating for them, particularly in view of the huge commitment in terms of their time, their energy, their homes, their money. They endeavoured to continue but found it too difficult. Their sense of hurt and loss is very deep.

14. Tallaght Youth Ministry Co-ordination Group

Background

This began as a network of local people involved in running youth ministry programmes in the various parishes in Tallaght. They were gathered initially in 1991 by the faith development team in the Catholic Youth Council (CYC) for a Christian leadership course, where they shared their experience, identified their needs and planned common actions in response to these. The network expanded in 1993 with the involvement of the Parish Development and Renewal team (PDR) along with the local bishop and clergy and the Tallaght Youth Service. A co-ordinating committee resulted from this, made up of representatives of local leaders, CYC, PDR and the Youth Service. The purpose of this committee is to keep an overview of youth ministry activities and to co-ordinate and support planning and implementation of youth ministry programmes in the 12 parishes in Tallaght.

Structure

A range of youth ministry programmes are running in most of the parishes, with the support of a local leadership. That leadership is represented in turn on the co-ordinating committee along with representatives of agencies interested in developing youth ministry. The committee meets about four times a year to plan its activities and organises common events for planning, training and celebrating.

Approach

A key element in the work of the committee has been the organisation of two youth-vision days. Teams were invited from each parish, helped to analyse the youth ministry needs in their area and put together a three year plan. A second day was organised where the teams met again, reported on progress in their parishes and their plans for the coming months. This co-ordinated planning and review allowed for much co-operation between the agencies and the locals. The co-ordinating committee organised training programmes in group skills. Each year they organise a Christmas party for all young people involved in their parishes, as a way of saying thank you for the work done.

On the ground, the parish teams are adopting a variety of approaches. Some are engaged with CYC and PDR in long-term planning with the millennium in mind. Others have taken on the *Cycle of Care* – a strategy for maintaining contact with a group of young people over a number of years – and are using such programmes as *Faith Friends, Gift* and *Inter-connect. Inter-connect* is a programme that establishes links with young people in the Third World and allows the young to share on their own experiences, on justice issues and scripture. Other parishes again are working with a range of individual programmes – *Faith Friends, Gift,* Advent, prayer evenings, a rock Mass, weekends in Glendalough, Christian rock concerts and others. A new programme currently being piloted is called *Bridges* – it is directed at adults to help them understand better changes in the church in the light of Vatican II and the changed experience of young people in the modern culture.

Reflections

The co-ordinated approach to youth ministry has affirmed and supported local youth ministry leaders. It gave them a place to share experiences and ideas, to offer and receive encouragement. It built up a sense of solidarity among the parish teams who up to then had been working in isolation. It created a good working relationship between the locals and the various agencies concerned with youth and ministry. This has facilitated the local teams in looking at needs together and in finding solutions together. It has empowered them to address their own youth ministry is-

sues. They are now confident enough to rewrite programmes to meet the needs of their particular situation.
All this in turn has led to a significant growth in youth
ministry activity on the ground.

Formation of adults has been crucial in all this, ensuring
future leaders and sustained development. This formation
has focused both on skills and faith development. The
committee is presently looking at ways of developing this
dimension of the training further.

PART 3

Frameworks for
Parish Youth Ministry

A Comprehensive Framework for Parish Youth Ministry

by Brendan Doyle

'Fully comprehensive' is not a term one would associate with young people or youth ministry. Normally 'fully comprehensive' is used in reference to motor insurance policies. In fact, if one was to use an insurance term for young people based on media reports, 'third party fire and theft' would be quite appropriate. It is unfair of course, that many young people are labelled as a risk, in the negative sense, because of the bad publicity given to a few. But a risk can also be positive. It can be a time for growth, a challenge, an opportunity for new life.

The attitude of 'Let's do something for young people – get them off the streets' is not an uncommon one. While the sentiments of the people behind this attitude might be good, their vision of young people and their potential are quite limited. Young people want to be treated as individuals and not labelled as 'a problem'. They want to be listened to and taken seriously. It is because of this that the Faith Development Team in CYC have developed a Comprehensive Framework for Parish Youth Ministry. By borrowing the term 'fully comprehensive', this framework gives a better and more positive sense to the embracing nature of youth ministry. Not only does it try to address the needs of young people, it involves them in the whole process and allows them to fully participate in the life of their community and wider society.

Components of a Comprehensive Framework

Because of the variety of young people in any given parish, different approaches need to be undertaken. Here is a list of components of a comprehensive framework of youth ministry. The questions which are posed under each heading, could act as a checklist for any parish or group trying to assess its services to its young people:

1. Evangelisation and Pre-Evangelisation

Evangelisation is about proclaiming the message of Christ. There are many ways this can happen. It might be by befriending young people, using a gospel-based drama at a youth gathering, inviting young people on a weekend, providing times for meditation, and so on.

Questions:

Is the parish community announcing the good news through lived example and by building up relationships with its young people?

Does it provide opportunities for young people to reflect on their life and on the Christian message?

2. Catechesis and Faith Development

This is helping young people to grow in their understanding of faith. This can be developed by providing opportunities for young people to talk and learn about their faith. It can be done through using a variety of different approaches, from retreats to programmes on certain themes, such as Advent, Lent, peace, social issues, etc., which enable people to reflect on what it means to be a Christian.

Question:

In what ways is the parish helping young people to grow in their Christian faith?

3. Christian Outreach

Christian outreach involves reaching out to young people who are alienated from church and social structures, those on the margins of society. It might mean anything from meeting young people where they congregate on the streets, to intensive one-to-one ministry. It could include responding to some of their basic needs, such as food and accommodation, helping them obtain basic skills for potential employment, counselling, receiving help for substance abuse, etc.

Question:
How is the parish reaching out to young people who are on the margins of its community and/or society?

4. Community Life

This is about building up a sense of community where young people feel that they belong and are a part of the community. It refers to events, projects and processes in which young people take on an active part. It may be a Summer Project, for example, where members of a parish, young and old, participate and enjoy various activities together.

Questions:
Are young people given an experience of belonging to a Christian community by participating in programmes, events or activities?
Does the parish support existing youth groups who are working for the good of their young people?

5. Enablement and Training

This entails empowering people to undertake a project, programme or a ministry in a given area. It is about encouraging people in their task as well as providing training where necessary so that people will feel competent enough. It is up to the parish at large to be enablers, talent spotters, so that various individuals can get an opportunity to grow in responsibility and develop their gifts.

Questions:
How are the leadership skills of young people and leaders

being supported and developed? Are young people empowered to work with their own peers?

Are leaders in the parish involved in any local or regional network of youth leaders which provides support, encouragement, exchange of ideas and work on some common projects like training or organising events, etc?

6. Prayer and Worship

This refers to young people preparing and participating in liturgies and developing their prayer life. These occasions can celebrate aspects of life and give people a time to rejoice and reflect on their lives.

Questions:

Are there opportunities for young people to deepen their relationship with Christ through prayer and liturgies that relate to their experiences?

7. Justice and Peace

This means encouraging young people to work for justice and peace not only in their own community but in the world. It may involve helping those in need in the local community, as well as heightening awareness of issues of injustices in other parts of the world and in some way trying to respond to them. Supporting Third World agencies in their work for justice, through 24 hour fasts, is one simple example of doing something on a wider scale for justice. This, in one way, would harness the energy of young people to do something to make the world a better place.

Question:

Is awareness of peace and justice issues promoted among young people?

8. Guidance

This concerns where, and to whom, young people can go for advice and support if they have a difficulty. It might mean having a handful of mature people who are good listeners and are available for young people to talk to. It could include training these 'listeners' in referral skills, so that young people could be referred to a specialised service if the need arose, or at least put in touch with groups such as Alanon, Alateen, Narcotics Anonymous, etc. Spiritual guidance would also be covered under this heading. Journeying with young people who wish to explore their faith questions is a very important element.

Questions:
Are there adults available for young people to talk to?
Is there an awareness among youth leaders of the specialised services available to meet particular needs of young people, for example, counselling for different situations young people find themselves in, Alanon, Alateen, Narcotics Anonymous, Cura, Bereavement groups, spiritual direction, etc?

9. Being a Voice for Young People
This ensures that someone speaks up for young people so they are not forgotten about or overlooked when decisions are being made that may affect them, such as in the case of parish councils or community hall committees, etc.

Questions:
Who speaks on behalf of young people on issues that affect them in the parish and the wider community?
Are young people fairly represented on parish committees etc?

These components highlight the diversity and gospel- inspired richness of such a vision for a parish. It is a 'fully comprehensive' framework from which a parish can work.

The task of going 'fully comprehensive' might seem daunting but, on reflection, many parishes are working on these elements but in an unco-ordinated and fragmented way. The inspiration behind such a framework or vision is that youth ministry is the responsibility of the whole parish or Christian community and not just one individual.

First Steps

The fundamental challenge of youth ministry is to do something, make a start. 'The longest journey begins with the first step.' (*Chinese proverb*) The next step will be to look at implementing a comprehensive framework for parish youth ministry.

Going Comprehensive

'People brought little children to him ... and the disciples turned them away. But Jesus said, "Let the children alone, and do not stop them coming to me; for it is to such as these that the kingdom of heaven belongs"' (Mt 19:13-15).

Youth ministry, that is, the Christian community's response to the needs of young people, is ultimately about introducing young people to Jesus. It is about introducing young people to the 'fullness of life' that Jesus came to bring. A comprehensive framework for youth ministry, initiated by a parish, involves the preparation and introduction of young people to Jesus, the nurturing of that relationship, and the living out of that relationship with the support of the Christian community. The question of how to implement this framework is the next focus.

The Co-ordinating Group

Because youth ministry is the responsibility of the whole parish or Christian community, it is important that a youth ministry co-ordinating group be established to oversee the implementation of a comprehensive framework. The composition of such a group would include people already involved in youth work and faith development initiatives in the parish. It is important that those selected have a wider vision of possibilities for young people than just their own project. Some people with little or no experience of working with young people, but with a genuine concern and willingness to work with them, would also be a good addition. A mixture of people, male and female, young and not so young, would bring balance and representation of the parish. It is preferable that fifty percent of the group be under the age of twenty five.

Tasks of the Co-ordinating Group

The tasks of the co-ordinating group are to co-ordinate and support what is already happening for young people in the parish, to examine the gaps in the parish's response to young people, and in some way to try to address these gaps by starting something new or by enlisting the help of others to do so.

The tasks of the group can be listed under three overall headings:
• Understanding young people.
• Having a vision of a comprehensive framework for
   parish youth ministry.
• Implementing a comprehensive framework.

Understanding Young People

It is very easy to brand young people as 'all the same' or to label them as 'difficult'. A necessary task of a co-ordinating group is to try and understand as much as possible about young people. An input or workshop on Adolescent and Faith Development, given by a fulltime youth worker/ catechist, would be a helpful resource to the group in understanding more about teenagers, as well as highlighting appropriate approaches and projects/programmes for particular age groups. Sometimes this type of input can help a group avoid the trap of presuming they know what is happening in the developmental life of young people, and therefore assuming they know what young people want.

Other items on the agenda of the group would be to look at the youth age-profile, as well as the different categories of young people in the parish.

In the recent past, the Faith Development Team of CYC have noted four different categories of young people that have come to their attention in their work with parishes. These categories highlight the broad spectrum of young people and the need for a variety of responses in any parish's plan for its young people:

1. The first category is young people who are already involved in the life of the parish. They may be in the folk group, be a Eucharistic minister, a minister of the Word, a faith friend, or a member of a discussion, liturgy or social action group.

2. The second category is those involved in non-parish groups such as sports and leisure clubs, drama groups, scouting and guide organisations, etc.

3. The third category is young people who are not involved in any organised grouping.

4. The fourth category is young people who tend to be isolated from their peers, even from their families. They tend to be 'loners' and keep to themselves. Even though this represents a very small percentage of young people, it is on the increase.

Having a Vision

The second overall area which a co-ordinating group needs to have a grasp of, is a comprehensive framework for parish youth ministry. This is a vision of what youth ministry could be in a parish. The nine components that make up this framework have already been outlined.

Implementation

The third overall area which the co-ordinating group must deal with is the implementation of a comprehensive framework of parish youth ministry.

This involves not only looking at what needs to happen, but what is already happening for young people in the parish. It involves listening and consulting with the youth in the parish. This can be done through a series of listening sessions with young people, organised especially for the older adolescent groupings. Or it could be done by incorporating consultation/listening sessions on young peoples' views in established youth programmes or groups already in the parish.

Before the group decides where to put its energy, the following questions need to be answered:

What is already happening for young people in the parish?

Do these need to be supported and encouraged by the parish?

What are the gaps or weaknesses in the parish's response to young people?

What can be done to address the weaknesses?

Does anything need to be initiated?

What help is needed to do this?

Are there resources that can be drawn upon?

Realistically, not everything can be 'taken on board' immediately, so it is up to the co-ordinating group to prioritise what needs to be done after addressing these questions.

The co-ordinating group can call on others in the parish to assist or initiate a specific project. An important function that might emerge in the group's works could be to convene a meeting of all those working with young people in the parish or area. A gathering like that would show what is happening for youth, as well as give people an opportunity to discuss needs and concerns, and possibly see if there are ways in which people could co-operate or work together in the future.

Assistance

The Faith Development Team in the Dublin diocese will provide a step-by-step approach to any parish wishing to set up a Co-ordinating Group and provide on-going practical support in the group's task. In many dioceses around the country there are fulltime youth directors co-ordinating youth ministry services for interested parishes. They would be more than happy to be of help. The task is daunting, but our young people deserve only our best efforts and not just our aspirations.

The Cycle of Care:
A Model for Parish Youth Ministry

by Peter Dorman and Brendan Doyle

The Cycle of Care is a five year parish youth ministry plan operating in the Dublin diocese. It begins with parishes working with children preparing for their confirmation, using the *Faith Friends* programme in a parish setting. When the programme is completed and the young people celebrate their confirmation, the parish organises follow-up programmes, events and activities for the young people over the next few years. By the time the twelve-year-olds reach the age of seventeen, they have experienced some sense of parish and belonging. They are then invited to become faith friends to the new twelve-year-olds preparing for confirmation, thus completing the Cycle of Care. By the end of the first five years, a pool of young leaders will hopefully have emerged. The project involves adults, young adults and young people throughout the various stages as it progresses over the five years. As each year passes the workload increases, so that there is something happening, not necessarily all at the same time, for the young people from the ages of 12 to 17 in the parish.

What is unique about the Cycle of Care is not necessarily the programmes or activities that are used over its duration, but the fact that it is a five year plan! It is the first time that a diocesan youth agency, along with a number of parishes and resource people, have together begun to plan and implement a long-term plan for parish youth ministry.

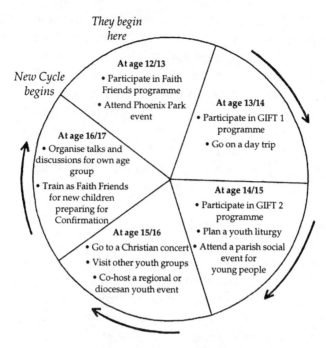

Figure 5: An example of the Cycle of Care five-year plan

Origins

The Cycle of Care was born out of the changing scene in youth ministry that has been emerging over the last seven or eight years. From the late 1970s to the late 1980s youth ministry was aimed at the 17 to 25 age group. The thinking was that, since there are already resources going into the younger age group through school catechetical programmes, the role of parishes should be to follow up when school is finished.

However, seventeen- to twenty-five-year-olds were and are becoming increasingly difficult to gather in parishes. This is most especially true where there has been no previous contact between the young people and parish. It seems unrealistic now to expect them to participate or get involved. In addition to that, there has been an increasing demand from parish workers for resources for the under seventeen age group. The demand has been particularly strong for the group aged 13 to 15. It seems that, overall, youth ministry programmes which were designed for young adults (17 to 25), such as discussion groups, youth liturgy groups, Taizé prayer groups, community service groups, etc., are being increasingly adopted by a 16 to 19 age group. The young adults are unfortunately moving out of the picture. The 13 to 15s, their appetite whet after *Faith Friends*, are crying out for more. In addition to that, many parishes are starting to actively reflect on the needs of their people. Many are getting organised to meet the challenges by putting planned strategies and structures in place. In terms of youth ministry, this is a welcome change from traditional practices. For too long the work has usually been left to the talented priest or sister or a keen volunteer. After an average period of three to five years, this individual is moved or burnt out, and the young people are left with a real sense of bereavement and often betrayal. Only if the parish as a whole takes responsibility and organises itself, can this be avoided.

Finally, with the establishment now of *Faith Friends* in many parishes, and the proliferation of short *Growing in Faith Together (Gift)* programmes later, the idea of following up on children after confirmation in a parish, not just in a school setting, is on the agenda. This represents a potential challenge to the now common reality of young people 'graduating' from the church at confirmation.

So what is all this saying? Or more accurately, what is the Spirit telling us through these changing realities? Simply, we believe it is this: It is no longer acceptable to parachute into the young adult world. Parishes need to organise themselves to journey in relationship with their young people from childhood to young adulthood. They need, at the very least, to be in touch, to have an open door to the young person at each stage of development along the way.

The Experience of Ballymun

The parish of the Virgin Mary in Ballymun is one parish which has struggled to meet these challenges. Under the stewardship of Fr Kevin O'Rourke, the parish worked to maintain contact with its young people after their confirmation programme. In the autumn of 1989, young people, mostly fifth-years from the comprehensive school, were taking part in a *Discovery* programme in the parish. Coming up to confirmation time, these young people were invited to act as confirmation faith friends to the candidates. Most accepted. The programme ran successfully, and these young leaders continued to organise activities after confirmation. In their first year at secondary school, the children were invited to join a parish youth club. Many did, and a number remained in St Pappin's youth club system until they were fifth-years themselves.

At this stage, they themselves participated in *Discovery* and subsequently trained as faith friends to the 1994 sixth class group. On the 25th of May 1994, they completed their *Faith Friends* programme, thus completing a cycle, beginning with their own confirmation where they were befriended by the fifth-years of 1989, and finishing in May when they did the same for their younger brothers and sisters. The completion of this cycle has been a momentous task. Simultaneously running parish programmes for confirmation candidates, plus first, second and third year clubs, plus *Discovery* and *Faith Friends* training, is a lot of work. Each year, following-up on last year adds to the work, but the rewards have been many.

Firstly, it generates its own pool of young leaders. At that time the parish was enjoying a glut of leadership: some fifty or sixty helpers aged 16 to 19 plus adult helpers had emerged through the process. Most importantly, the structure creates a skeleton of youth ministry in the parish to which much can be attached. At a drop of a hat, all the

young people involved can be brought off on a parish retreat. The quality of relationship and trust established between the youth and the parish is such that it enables it to
move forward with faith development programming that
would be unthinkable where there was no such relationship. Seeing what has been possible in Ballymun, which
we have called The Cycle of Care, the Faith Development
Team of CYC extended and promoted this model in a way
that is practical for other parishes.

Diocesan Launch

After research of and consultation with a good cross-section of parishes and leaders, The Faith Development Team
of the CYC launched the Cycle of Care in the Autumn of
1994. The criteria used by the team for parishes wishing to
participate in the training which would prepare them to
run the Cycle were:

1. Parishes can participate if they run *Faith Friends* using a
parish-based training core group, or are willing to set one
up. It is not enough that one person runs the programme
in isolation or that it is a school-based programme.

2. Parishes must be willing to follow-up the *Faith Friends*
programme.

3. Parishes must be willing to network with other parishes,
not only during the training course but at evaluation and
planning meetings later on.

4. Parish staff must be behind the project.

It was hoped that ten parishes would pilot the project, but
seventeen signed up instead!

Parishes were encouraged to set up a core group of between five and eight people, to include a mix of young and
not so young, a member of the parish staff or someone
with the official backing of the parish, and some existing
Faith Friends, if the programme is already used in the
parish.

Out of the seventeen parishes chosen, nine had confirmation dates between February and Easter (April) and the remaining eight had dates after Easter. Training began for the set of nine parish core-groups in November, and the second set the following January.

All the groups underwent ten hours of training over five evenings. The training included team building, analysing and adapting *Faith Friends* material for each parish, planning the recruiting and training of faith friends at home, and taking on board the vision of the Cycle of Care. After the training, each parish core group recruited and trained faith friends in the their own parish and ran the programme with the children preparing for confirmation. The core groups evaluated the programme with their faith friends and then went to a gathering of all the other parish core groups in May 1995 to review, share experiences and celebrate the first year of the Cycle of Care. A giant outdoor event, consisting of orienteering and an open air concert for all the children and faith friends, was organised for the seventeen parishes in the Phoenix Park in June. This acted as a culmination to all the parish activities and programmes held during the year and served as a diocesan get-together, highlighting the wider nature of the church in Dublin.

For year two of the Cycle, a general information night was held in September 1995 for the seventeen parishes plus others who were interested in the Cycle. The night gave an opportunity for core groups to re-group but also to hear about the many follow-up options they could engage in to keep in contact with the children who had made their confirmation earlier that year. Training and help was offered on the various options and most groups signed up for one or more. Others had existing programmes, such as *Gift*, in their parish so they directed the children to these. Some core groups were still at full strength while others recruited a number of their faith friends to their depleted ranks. A small number had to be content with what they were left with but still kept a look out for new members.

In quite a few cases the core groups divided in two, one following-up the children from year one and the other concentrating on the new children preparing for confirmation.

By the end of year two of the Cycle, the majority of parishes had followed-up with the young people as well as implementing another *Faith Friends* programme for the new children making their confirmation. Also by then a further thirteen parishes were following the Cycle of Care model and were invited to bring their children to the second outdoor gathering of young people and faith friends in the Phoenix Park in June 1996.

Year three of the Cycle began in September 1996 with an information night on initiatives to follow up children from years one and two of the Cycle. A handful of parishes have already introduced a small core group to co-ordinate a specific year in the Cycle so that by the end of the five years there will be five small core groups in place to oversee the project.

During May 1997 a detailed evaluation of the Cycle of Care was conducted with each parish core group. A general meeting for all the parish core groups was held at the end of that month to present the findings. This meeting was focused on what steps were needed for the Cycle of Care to continue in each parish and what assistance, if any, was required.

In June, the third annual outing to the Phoenix Park took place for all the parishes involved in the Cycle.

By the end of year three, 90% of the parishes were still implementing year 1 of the Cycle; 70% were implementing years 1 and 2; and 50% were implementing years 1, 2 and 3 of the Cycle. (See the figure opposite.)

September 1997 saw the beginning of year 4 of the Cycle with emphasis being placed on encouraging parishes to follow up the children, especially after years 2 and 3. A choice of activities, programmes, events and training was offered to parishes so that this could be facilitated. This will be repeated in early 1998 to accomodate groups with a later timetable. A special Christmas fun event for young people was organised by young people in years 3 and 4 and was hosted by one of the parishes, with help from CYC. Interest has already been expressed in holding a similar event in Lent, possibly on the theme of methods of prayer.

Cycle of Care Five-Year Plan
Example of a parish plan

	Year 1	Year 2	Year 3	Year 4	Year 5
16/17 Years					Discovery Programme Train as Faith Friends
15/16 Years				GIFT 3 *or* Advent *or* Lent programme Attend a Christian concert	GIFT 3 *or* Advent *or* Lent programme Attend a Christian concert
14/15 Years			GIFT 2 A youth liturgy Social event	GIFT 2 A youth liturgy Social event	GIFT 2 A youth liturgy Social event
13/14 Years		GIFT 1 *or* Interconnect A day outing	GIFT 1 *or* Interconnect A day outing	GIFT 1 *or* Interconnect A day outing	GIFT 1 *or* Interconnect A day outing
12/13 Years	Faith Friends Phoenix Park Event	Faith Friends Phoenix Park Event	Faith Friends Phoenix Park Event	Faith Friends Phoenix Park Event	Faith Friends Phoenix Park Event

The Learnings so far

Vision

Keeping the vision of the Cycle of Care to the forefront in each parish is vital. The Cycle may mean initiating new projects each year, but it might also mean incorporating existing youth groups into the plan so that the young people can choose from a range of activities and programmes available. Some of these existing groups may not have been considered beforehand because of the lack of a 'faith element' in their work with youth. It is important that follow-up with the children has a mixture of faith sharing and discussion, recreational and educational work to choose from, so that as many young people as possible can avail of what the parish is offering throughout their teenage years. A bringing together of all the youth groups and/or leaders to highlight what is on offer for young people in a given parish is a worthwhile exercise and can even act as an overall co-ordinating venture.

Volunteers

There is always the danger of overburdening volunteers, or frightening them off with long-term commitments. The balancing act throughout the process is to extend the work without overburdening volunteers. This could be achieved by inviting people to make limited but renewable commitments, from which they can extract themselves after agreed periods. The Cycle of Care is a tall order, and an entire five year plan cannot be bitten off in one mouthful.

If all the core group, for example, opt out, it is back to the drawing board for the co-ordinator or convener to find new people to form a core group and have them trained to run a particular programme. This is a daunting task, but it is spreading the responsibility for the young back to the community. The *Faith Friends* programme is drawing upon the early church experience where a community 'walked' with new potential members over a period of time.

Maintenance of Cycle

Maintaining the Cycle in a parish demands commitment, on-going evaluation, and an openness to new initiatives as they arise. What is also crucial is the backing of the parish staff, regular recruitment of volunteers, and assistance, support and training from the diocesan youth ministry team.

Feedback

One of the most interesting reactions to the Cycle of Care Project has come from young adults, who have told us that at an earlier age they took part as children in the *Faith Friends* programme or as members of a youth club or summer project or prayer groups, and that now they have come full circle and are now leaders to the new generation of younger adolescents. It was not planned, but it was a natural outcome to their on-going participation in the life of their grouping or parish.

Conclusion

The Cycle of Care gives parishes a unique opportunity to work with young people in a co-ordinated and developmental way. Its ultimate purpose is to provide young people with a sense of belonging and purpose as members of a caring Christian community, so that they in turn can proclaim the message of Christ in a relevant, hope-filled and life-giving way for others.

'We meant what we said!'
Affirming the Cycle of Care

by Bishop Donal Murray

As the confirmation season approaches, uncomfortable questions make themselves felt once again. For many twelve-year-olds, the sacrament does not mark the beginning of an adult, active involvement in the life of the church; it marks the beginning of a lengthy, perhaps permanent, withdrawal from religious practice and from participation in parish life.

At one time, confirmation was almost invariably spoken of in terms of making young people 'strong and perfect Christians' or 'soldiers of Christ'. In the earlier part of this century it was often called 'the sacrament of Catholic Action'. Nowadays, it is most commonly described as the sacrament of commitment.

Commitment is indeed important in the person being confirmed. Young people are challenged to commit themselves: they promise to use generously and courageously the gifts and fruits of the Holy Spirit. Their commitment, like our own, is often lived out with less than their whole heart and soul and mind. But the real cause for worry is that, however wise or courageous or loving or committed they may be in other ways, so many confirmed young people appear to have little or no connection with the life of the church community.

Peter Dorman's article, 'The Cycle of Care, A New Model for Youth Ministry', in CYC's newsletter *Update*, prompted me to reflect on the meaning of confirmation from a slightly different angle. There is another commitment involved in confirmation. There is the commitment made by the parish and the wider church community.

Like every sacrament, confirmation is an act of the church. The church rejoices because some of its members are receiving the Holy Spirit as the apostles did at Pentecost. It welcomes them as people sent to bear witness to the truth of Christ.

What is expressed in the sacraments is a truth which is also an obligation. We have a duty to mean what we say and to do what we say. The church, for instance, expresses her care for the sick in anointing, or her support for the bride and groom in marriage. Each community and each member is called to translate that care and support into practical action.

The whole parish community, and each member of it, has a responsibility to make the church's recognition of the mission and gifts of newly confirmed members a living reality. The community needs to show that recognition in the way it welcomes, supports and challenges its young people.

There are, no doubt, important questions to be asked about the nature of youth culture – the difficulties it raises and the opportunities it provides for Christian commitment. It may be desirable to look at ways in which schools could more effectively support students in living out their commitment. There is much that could be done in helping parents to help their teenagers to grow in faith in an increasingly difficult environment.

None of these questions can substitute for the challenge that is posed to parishes: 'How can this parish welcome, support and inspire those who have been confirmed?' On confirmation day, the girls and boys are told that we thank God for the gifts of the Holy Spirit which they receive; they are told that these gifts are vital in the life of the church; they are told that their parents, sponsors, friends and neighbours are praying that they may use their gifts well. Some weeks or months down the line, how would we respond to a young person who challenged us to show what all of that actually amounted to in terms of practical action?

In the document which followed the Synod of Bishops devoted to the topic of catechesis, Pope John Paul put it as follows:

> Catechesis runs the risk of becoming barren if no community of faith and Christian life takes the catechumen in at a certain stage of his catechesis. That is why the ecclesial community at all levels has a twofold responsibility with regard to catechesis: it has the responsibility of providing for the training of its members, but it also has the responsibility of welcoming them into an environment where they can live as fully as possible what they have learned. (*Catechesi Tradendae*, 24)

Anyone who looks at the situation of young people after confirmation, can scarcely fail to hear the challenge that is implied in those words. Where are teenagers to find the ecclesial community which welcomes them into an environment where they can live as fully as possible what they have learned? If they cannot find such a community, catechesis risks becoming barren.

Over-reliance on the school environment is bound to set up the situation in which school leavers find themselves suddenly in an environment which they do not see as challenging and supporting their commitment. If the parish environment seems unchallenging and unsupportive while they are at school, it is hardly likely to appear otherwise simply because they have left school.

The initiatives mentioned in the article on the Cycle of Care are pastorally very promising – the *Gift* programme, the *Discovery* programme, the extension of contact with *Faith Friends* into the years of post-primary education. It is good that the Faith Development Team is involved in seeing what can actually be done. While we can all recognise the needs, what is often required is a concrete illustration of how real-life parishes are actually meeting those needs.

The Cycle of Care responds to the very meaning of confirmation seen as a sacrament of commitment by the parish to its younger members. It is about the parish community accepting its responsibility to be an environment in which people can live as fully as possible what they have learned. It is about a parish community taking concrete steps to give practical expression to what it has celebrated. It is about a parish saying to its people, 'We meant what we said.'

That is a necessary complement to the commitment of the young people to the parish and to the mission of the church. If their commitment is to flourish, it requires an environment in which they can live what they have learned. The primary school which they are leaving, cannot provide that environment for them. The post-primary school can do a certain amount, but with the best will in the world it cannot do everything. The rest of the student's environment, what they may think of as 'the real world', must also be seen by them as a place calling for commitment. For this reason, the cycle must be one not simply of care but of challenge. Young parishioners, several times during their young adult years, should be brought face to face with needs and the possibilities, both within the parish and further afield; they should be offered some indications of the ways in which they might respond. They should be allowed the possibility of discussing and meeting needs and opportunities which they might themselves identify. There is no one way of doing that – personal contact, exhibitions and publicity about parish activities, folk groups and prayer groups – there are many possibilities. Creating a cycle of challenge could be an expression of the mission of committed young people to their contemporaries.

A parish in which the Cycle of Care was really operating would not see the confirmation ceremony simply as a commitment made by the young people being confirmed. It would understand that it was a commitment by the parish to these young people, a commitment to be the ecclesial community which welcomes them and confirms them in their faith.

The parish, to put it in Pope John Paul's words, must rediscover its vocation, which is to be a 'welcoming family home, where those who have been baptised and confirmed become aware of forming the People of God. In that home, the bread of good doctrine and the Eucharistic Bread are broken in abundance, in the setting of the one act of worship; from that home they are sent out day by day to their apostolic mission in all the centres of activity of the life of the world.' (*Catechesi Tradendae*, 67)

Some points of good practice identified by the project leaders

• There is a clear value in giving people a definite, limited and achievable task to do in their own area. It offers them a role, and it allows them to take ownership and responsibility for youth ministry in their own parishes. It also allows the parish to see in advance what is being asked of it and what commitment is required.

• Just as volunteers need nourishment to sustain their commitment, so too do the fulltimers need space for reflection and renewal. A stressed-out youth minister is not good for the work.

• Key to the development of new programmes, and the training of teams to run them, is a continuous process of evaluating the programmes – an evaluation that includes all the participants – which results in the continuous rewriting of the packages in the light of experience.

• The values of formation, evaluation and networking are central to making youth ministry experiences available to the widest possible number of young people.

• By and large, local groups of volunteers need at least the passive support of local clergy, and where this is absent the groups generally do not survive. A diocesan agency cannot provide this local support role.

• Confidence building among volunteers is as crucial as training them in the details of programmes.

• Diocesan policy on youth ministry, if it is to be efficient and effective, needs to be practically integrated with the overall diocesan pastoral policy.

• The practice of bringing in outside facilitators for overall ministly planning and assessment works well.

• Covenanting is a very concrete way of involving lay people in the ownership of youth ministry.

• Fulltime staff hold planning and review meetings every two weeks – reviewing work done over the previous two weeks and planning ahead for the next two – has proved an effective and efficient structure.

• Collaboration among neighbouring parishes and groups in the training of youth and adult leaders has proved very practical and workable. It has, on the whole, maintained and developed energy for youth ministry in the areas without becoming a burden for those involved.

• The basic strategy of running only with programmes for which their was adult commitment worked well. It was a very concrete way of offering adults in a community responsibility for ministry to their young. It also meant that an already overworked parish staff were not further burdened with having to organise and run programmes. Instead they could put their energy into the overall co-ordination.

• A planned co-ordinated approach to youth ministry can lay the basis for a comprehensive ministry. However, a crucial need here is somebody to take up the co-ordination role.

• A youth ministry centre, with a homely and relaxed atmosphere, makes it is easier to create a sense of ease where the young people – particularly those from difficult backgrounds – are able to share and find a listening ear.

• People hunger for spirituality, if it is presented in a digestible form. Personal development and artistic programmes provide doors into the spiritual.

• The key to effective youth ministry is giving young people ownership. Educating young people to run something is better than doing it for them. They grow in confidence and there is more energy and creativity all around. It avoids dependency on a few adult leaders, leadership burn-out and the collapse of the organisation. The young people taking on responsibilities offer models for the younger ones coming up.

• Young people in oppressed areas easily identify with oppression in other cultures.

• Young people need to belong to a group if they are to be supported in their choice of an alternative lifestyle.

• Bringing young people to other cultures/countries is very energising for them and provides great opportunity for general training and planning skills.

• While there is often a resistance among young people to organised religion, there is an openness to spirituality and to practical Christianity. Hence actions around Third World issues, joy riding, etc., can be very successful. In this context, discussion about values and spirituality can be informal but engaging – arising naturally in the context of the activities.

• It helps to put programme leaders working in pairs – an experienced person with a newer person

• It is important to hold regular celebratory events for volunteers as a way of saying thank you for the work done.

• Close liaison between schools and parish is a vital element in the development of a comprehensive parish youth ministry.

• Continuity in the relationship between leaders and young people contributes greatly to the building up of trust and friendship.

• A programme mixture that includes faith development, personal development and leadership skills is vital for bringing new leaders on stream.

Glossary of Terms and Programmes

Comhairle: Comhairle Leas óige
Youth service of the Dublin city Vocational Education Committee.

Covenanting
A system of funding whereby individuals agree to a regular debit in their account in favour of a designated youth ministry.

CYC: Catholic Youth Council
The Dublin diocesan youth agency. This includes a Faith Development Team who provide back-up support for parish youth ministry across the diocese. Address: Arran Quay, Dublin 7. Phone: (01) 872 5055.

Cycle of Care
A structured five-year parish plan for youth ministry involving young people between the ages of 12 and 17 and run by a trained parish youth ministry team. Further details from CYC Faith Development team.

Discovery
A parish based young adult programme with talks and small group discussions on topics related to faith and life. Further details from The Columba Press, 55A Spruce Avenue, Stillorgan Industrial Park, Blackrock, Co Dublin. Tel 01 2942560

Do you know it is Advent?
A short programme for young adults exploring advent themes. Available from the Catholic Youth Council.

Enjoy praying
A small group programme on praying published by
Family Caring Trust. 44 Rathfriland Rd, Newry, Co Down,
BT34 1LD. Tel 01693 64174

Faith Friends
Small group programme based on friendship and faith
sharing for children preparing for 1st Communion and
Confirmation and facilitated by young adults. Further details from The Columba Press, 55A Spruce Avenue,
Stillorgan Industrial Park, Blackrock, Co Dublin. Tel 01
2942560

Gift: Growing in Faith Together
A series of published discussion programmes for 1st, 2nd
and 3rd year students. Small groups meet on weekly basis,
facilitated by an adult. Covers a range of topics on life and
faith. Further details from Veritas, Middle Abbey St.
Dublin 1.

Inter-connect
A six-session programme for post-confirmation young
people on issues of justice and injustice, involving links
between young people in Ireland and in developing countries. Further details from CYC Faith Development Team.
Telephone 01 872 5055

Listening survey
A small group discussion programme with young people
of the same age. They meet one hour a week for four
weeks or so to talk about the following: what are young
people of your age angry ... sad ... hurt ... worried ... delighted about? The discussion is facilitated by two adults
who record the issues. The material gathered is used to
plan youth ministry. Further details from Martin Kennedy.
Tel 087 608326

Love matters
A programme on sex education written by Francis
McCrickard and published by Veritas.

Make me a Channel of your Peace
A twelve-week published programme for 16+ year olds including talks, prayer and discussion that seeks to help young people recognise their gifts. Further details from Michael and Maire McCracken, 5 Lomond Heights, Cookstown, BT 80 8XW. Tel 016487 63483

PDR: Parish Development and Renewal
A Dublin diocesan agency consisting of a team of fulltime workers which offers back-up support to parishes engaged in development or renewal work.

Peer Ministry
The term generally designates any youth ministry programme that is run by or with young people.

Taizé
An ecumenical monastery in the south of France visited every year by thousands of young people across Europe. It has inspired the setting up of hundreds of Taizé-style prayer meetings and liturgies across Ireland. For details on an annual pilgrimage to Taizé contact the Catholic Youth Council.

Taking Charge of Your Life
A programme in assertiveness training for young adults, run over a series of nights. Published by Family Caring Trust, 44 Rathfriland Rd, Newry, Co Down BT34, lLD. Tel 01693 64174

Weeks of Directed Prayer
A one-to-one ministry in prayer mentoring where participants follow a daily programme of prayer accompanied by a meeting with a trained mentor or *anam chara*. For further information contact the Adult Prayer Ministry Team, Seafield House, 123 Cill Eoin Road, Cill Eoin, Rostrevor BT 34 3AQ.

Youth Fairs Day
A public information event where young young people

are invited to view stands and displays set up in a central venue by clubs, societies and organisations interested in recruiting youth. For further details contact Shay Claffey, Parochial House, Tullamore, Co Offaly. Tel 0506 21587

Youth Link
Northern Ireland Youth Inter-Church training resource. Further details from Fr Paddy White, 143A University St, Belfast BT7, Tel 01232 323217

Youth Service
Statutorily funded youth work, franchised mainly to youth organisations to run.